Ring Around the Hexies

42½'' x 42½''

PIECED BY BONNIE K. HUNTER AND MICKEY DEPRE
MACHINE QUILTED BY MICKEY DEPRE

Ring Around the Hexies

A Collaboration Celebration

By Bonnie K. Hunter and Mickey Depre
Editor: Deb Rowden
Designer: Kelly Ludwig
Photography: Aaron T. Leimkuehler
Illustration: Eric Sears
Technical Editor: Jane Miller
Photo Editor: Jo Ann Groves

Published by:
Kansas City Star Books
1729 Grand Blvd.
Kansas City, Missouri, USA 64108
All rights reserved
Copyright © 2013 Bonnie K. Hunter, Mickey Depre, and The Kansas City Star Co.

First edition, first printing
ISBN: 978-1-61169-108-5
Library of Congress Control Number: 2013948931
Printed in the United States of America by Walsworth Publishing Co., Marceline, MO

To order copies, call StarInfo at (816) 234-4473 and say "Books."

The Quilter's Home Page

www.PickleDish.com

Contents

Introduction

What do you get when you cross passionately pieced scrappy quilts with vibrant Pieced Hexies? A Collaboration Celebration!

In the pages to come, we share our love of fabric, and our passion for color and creative design in a project that lets both of our worlds collide into something that is wonderfully challenging, yet easier than it looks.

Bonnie K. Hunter's easy machine piecing creates a scrap lover's background "canvas" perfectly suited to showcase Mickey Depre's wonderful Pieced Hexie rosettes. It's a match made in fabric-heaven!

Get ready for Ring Around the Hexies!

About the Authors

Bonnie K. Hunter is passionate about quilting, focusing mainly on scrap quilts with the simple feeling of "making do." She started her love affair with quilting in home economics class during her senior year of high school in 1980 and has never looked back. Bonnie is the author of several Kansas City Star Quilt Books — *Scraps & Shirttails*, *Scraps & Shirttails II*, *Adventures with Leaders & Enders*, and *String Fling* — with more to come. Catch up with Bonnie's daily doings on her website and blog: Quiltville.com.

Bonnie and her husband, Dave, are the proud parents of two grown sons, Jason and Jeffrey. They round out their household with Sadie, the dog, and two cats — Emmy Lou, who loves life inside only, and Chloe, who only loves life on the outside — keeping Bonnie company while she designs, quilts, and plays happily with her fabric.

Bonnie's favorite motto? "The best things in life are quilted!" Of course!

Mickey Depre was introduced to the world of fiber arts at the age of four by her own personal "grand masters." Grandmothers, great aunts, aunts and her mother filled her days with cloth, needles, yarn and such. In 1997, she found quilting on her own.

Mickey made a name for herself as an art quilter with a flair for the whimsical, but always made traditional quilts for her husband, Paul Sr., and children, Paul Jr. and Emily, to enjoy and keep warm under.

English Paper Piecing has become her new obsession and led to the publication of her book, *Pieced Hexies*. Mickey's motto: "There is more than enough fabric in my studio to be both an art quilter and a traditional quilter."

Advice from Bonnie

I **love playing with blocks that** leave space to showcase Mickey Depre's Pieced Hexie rosettes! I am a huge fan of on-point settings, and this one with wide-open alternate blocks creates a "place to land" for the Hexie rosettes. I also love pieced setting triangles that frame all of the excitement clear to the outside edge.

No border is necessary, but one could be added if you wish to make the quilt bigger.

A bit about the way I work:

As a scrap quilter, I work by unit size. Use whatever technique you wish to make half-square triangles for your quilt.

Note: When I say **unfinished**, that is what the unit measures **before** it is sewn into the block or quilt. The **finished** measurement is the final size of the unit (when all the seam allowances have been sewn).

Supply List

Our yardage requirements **use the** version shown here as a guide. We went with a scrappy approach, as you'll see in the quilt photo. You can go this route or use a single fabric for each color if this is more to your liking.

You can make this wallhanging project in any colorway you wish. Just substitute your choices with the colors listed below to be sure you have enough yardage.

Please read through the entire yardage supply list before cutting any fabrics.

Blue/Purple/Orange/Lilac/Black Version

Purple: 9 different dark purple prints, ⅝ yard total for star points and cornerstones

Orange (yellows/golds)**:** 9 fat eighths of yellow/gold/orange prints - ¾ yard total for block centers, cornerstones, and border triangles

Black: 1 yard of solid black for the Pieced Hexie rosette block backgrounds and pieced setting triangles

Lilac: ½ yard for star block backgrounds

Blue: 1¼ yards of blue check or print

Additional borders and bindings as desired!

Fabric for Hexies: If you make your Hexie rosettes in the same fabric choices as the background, you will have enough scraps to use from the yardage listed above.

or

If you wish to make your Hexie rosettes with different fabrics, you need at least 5 to 6 fat eighths (or equivalent) of desired fabrics.

Other Supplies Needed

Sewing machine, thread, needles, pins, scissors, seam ripper, small mat, rotary cutter, ruler.

For Pieced Hexies

- ❂ 28 – 1½" paper hexagons (available at Paper Pieces.com)
- ❂ Silk thread or a high quality cotton thread (neutral color) for hand sewing.
- ❂ Coordinating needles (Sharps/Applique/Milliners/Straw) that match your choice of sewing thread
- ❂ Thread for basting (any color, will not be in the finished project)
- ❂ Spray starch (I highly recommend Best Press.)
- ❂ Small ruler (either 4" or 3½" square)
- ❂ Fine tip pen or sharpened pencil
- ❂ Thimble
- ❂ TRI TOOL Ruler (ezQuilting/Tri Recs Tools by Darlene Zimmerman and Joy Hoffman www.simplicity.com)

Piecing the Quilt Top

Collaboration Star Block — 10" finished

Cutting Instructions

For each of the 9 blocks cut:

- ❂ 1 - 2" x 9" purple rectangle
- ❂ 16 - 2" purple squares
- ❂ 2 - 2" x 9" lilac rectangles
- ❂ 4 - 2" x 4½" lilac rectangles
- ❂ 4 - 2" x 4½" blue rectangles
- ❂ 1 - 2" x 9" orange rectangle
- ❂ 1 - 4½" orange square

Repeat 9 times to make 9 blocks. We used 2 different purples in each block - one in the four-patches and one as the star points.

Block 1

- ❂ Each block requires 4 - four-patches.
- ❂ Match a purple and lilac 2" x 9" strip with right sides together. Press seam toward the purple.
- ❂ Match an orange and a lilac 2" x 9" strip with right sides together. Press seam toward the orange.
- ❂ Sub-cut each pair of strips into 4 - 2" sections. Join sections as shown to make 4 corner four-patches. Press.

Star Point Units

Draw diagonal lines on the back of 16 purple 2" squares.

Upper Star Points

Place a purple square at each end of a lilac 2" x 4½" rectangle, watching which way the diagonals run. Stitch, folding back the square along the seam line to be sure it meets the edges of the rectangle. If it does, clip excess fabric ¼" away from seam line. Make 4, pressing seams toward the purple triangles.

Lower Star Points

Place a purple square at each end of a blue 2" x 4½" rectangle, watching which way the diagonals run. Stitch, folding back the square along the seam line to be sure it meets the edges of the rectangle. If it does, clip excess fabric ¼" away from seam line. Make 4, pressing seams toward the blue base rectangle.

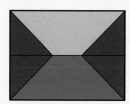

Join the star point halves together, nesting the seams. Press to one side.

Lay out the pieces for the block as shown, adding a center 4½" orange square that matches the orange fabric in the four-patches.

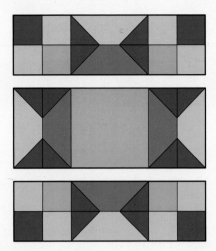

Assemble the block into rows, joining the rows to complete one block. Press. Make 9 blocks.

Alternate Block — 10" finished

Cutting Instructions for 4 blocks

- ✪ 16 - 2" x 7½" black rectangles
- ✪ 4 - 7½" black squares
- ✪ 16 - 2" orange squares (my fabrics are ALL scrappy!)

Assembly

Join an orange square to each end of 8 of the black rectangles, pressing seams toward the black rectangles.

Stitch a black 2" x 7½" black rectangle to either side of the 4 - 7½" black squares. Press seams toward the rectangles just added. (Note: image is shown in gray to show the seam lines.)

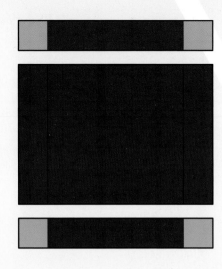

Add pieced rectangles to either end of the pieced center section, pressing seams toward the outer rectangles. Make 4 blocks.

Pieced Setting Triangles

Note: There are many commercial cutting methods for cutting half-square triangles - use any method that gives you a 2" finished half square triangle. Plan your yardage according to the method you plan to use.

Cutting Instructions

- ✪ 30 - 2⅞" orange squares
- ✪ 30 - 2⅞" black squares
- ✪ 2 - 2⅞" black squares cut on the diagonal once (from corner to corner)
- ✪ 8 - 2½" black squares

Assembly

Match orange and black 2⅞" squares with right sides together and cut on the diagonal once (from corner to corner) to yield 60 matched pairs. Stitch, pressing seams toward the black fabric. Units measure 2½" and finish at 2" in the quilt.

Make 60. Press seams toward the orange fabric.

Setting Triangles

Cutting Instructions

- ⊗ 5 - 3¼" orange squares
- ⊗ 5 - 3¼" black squares
- ⊗ 2 - 9¾" blue squares
- ⊗ 2 - 5⅛" blue squares

Assembly

Black on left *Black on right*

Match orange 3¼" squares with black 3¼" squares with right sides together. Cut them twice on the diagonal to yield 20 quarter-square triangle pairs.

Make 12 "half-hour glass" units with black on the right and 8 "half-hour glass" units with black on the left as shown.

Left side pieced unit *Right side pieced unit*

Using 8 of the "black on left" half-hour glass units and 3 half square triangles, make 8 left side pieced units.

Using 8 of the "black on right" half-hour glass units, 3 half square triangles, and one black square, make 8 right side pieced units.

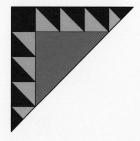

Stack the 9¾" blue squares and cut diagonally twice to make 8 large setting triangles.

Stack the 5⅛" blue squares and cut them once on the diagonal to yield 4 corner triangles.

Sew a left side pieced unit to the left side of the large triangle, pressing the seam toward the triangle.

Complete the unit by adding the right side pieced unit to the top, also pressing the seam toward the blue triangle. Make 8.

Corner Triangles

Using the remaining 4 half-hour glass units with black on right, piece 4 corner sections as shown.

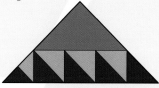

Add a small blue corner triangle to each section, pressing the seam toward the blue triangle. Make 4.

Assembly Diagram

Lay out the pieced blocks and alternate blocks as shown, filling in the outside edges with the setting triangles and corners. This on-point setting is assembled in diagonal rows.

Bonnie likes to piece diagonally set quilts into two halves. (One half will contain the center row and be larger than the remaining half.) Join quilt top halves to complete quilt center. Press seams toward the alternate blocks.

Making the Hexies

Hexies are a new technique for working with English paper piecing and hexagons. You need a paper template - we provide one on the next page. Follow the instructions below to make your Hexie – then to attach 7 Hexies to make a rosette to appliqué onto your quilt top. We do assume you know how to do English paper piecing – full instructions are provided in Mickey's 2012 book, *Pieced Hexies*.

Boomer

Boomer is a special design that steps away from using a 3½" square as the base by piecing a very loose triangle block to cover your paper Hexie. Mickey uses the TRI TOOL ruler (see supplies, page 6). Tools are good - they can make quilting very easy and very creative. Don't worry - this design is truly simple to do.

As always, the center hexagon is a solid fabric – no piecing instructions are needed.

Material Needed for 1 Hexie

- ✪ Fabric A: (1) 1¾" x 4"
- ✪ Fabric B: (1) 2¼" x 4"
- ✪ Fabric C: (2) 1¼" x 4"

Fabric Preparation

- ✪ Sew A lengthwise to B.
- ✪ Place the block in front of you with the B fabric on the bottom.
- ✪ Use the TRI TOOL Ruler as shown on the next page to create a triangle shape. Place the ruler

so the 3¾" line is even with the bottom edge of your block and trim.

- ✪ Sew C across the lengthwise edge of the A/B unit on each side (see finished block graphic).

OR

Material Needed for 1 Rosette (see page 13)

- ✪ Fabric A: (1) 1¾" x 25"
- ✪ Fabric B: (1) 2¼" x 25"
- ✪ Fabric C: (12) 1¼" x 4"
- ✪ Center: 3½" square

Fabric Preparation

- ✪ **Important** - Trim pieced seams to ⅛" after each one is sewn. This will reduce the bulk for basting.

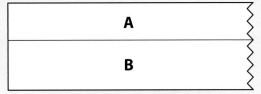

Trim pieced seams.

- ✪ Sew A lengthwise to B.
- ✪ Place the A/B strip in front of you with the B fabric on the bottom.

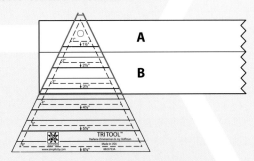

- Use the TRI TOOL Ruler to trim the triangle shape. Place the ruler so the 3¾" line is even with the bottom edge of your block.

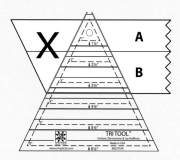

- Move the ruler down the strip and cut the remaining 5 identical triangles. **Note:** the triangle marked with the "X" is scrap. Set aside.

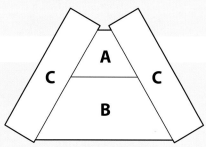

Boomer sewn triangle block

- Sew C across the lengthwise edge of the A/B unit on each side.

Paper Preparation

- Now baste the sewn square to the paper pattern. Perfect alignment is important - mark your paper hexagon with the alignment guides shown. Use a sharp pointed pencil or a fine tip pen to mark lines. To mark accurately, angle your marking instrument tip into the groove of the ruler and paper.

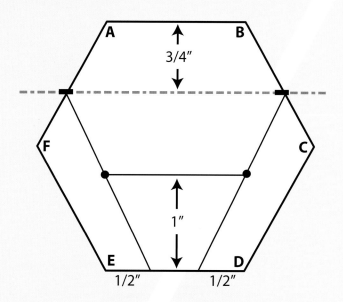

Layer Alignment Guides

Refer to this guide for the orientation of labeled corners A to F. No need to mark these letters on your Hexie paper.

- Measure ¾" horizontally down from the top edge of the Hexie (between points A and B) and make a mark at each side of the Hexie (between F and A, B and C) as indicated by the heavy tick mark on the graphic. Measure ½" to the right of corner E and left of corner D and mark. Draw a line connecting the marks from F to E and C to D.

- Measure 1" from the bottom (edge between corners E and D) and draw across from previous drawn lines.

Assembly

- Place the sewn triangle with the seam side facing up.

- Place the marked paper pattern on top of the sewn triangle with markings facing up.

- Line up the sewn seams and paper marks. Carefully pin once in the center, securing the sewn square to the paper. *Note: stick a pin vertically through the drawn line intersection to the check alignment of the sewn intersection. Pin should go thru fabric intersection of A-B-C on each side.*

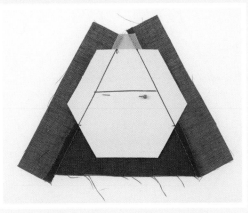

⊗ Trim away excess fabric, leaving a generous ¼"
on each side for basting.

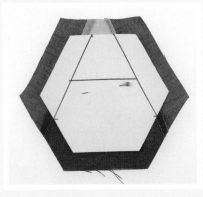

⊗ Baste the sewn square to the paper hexagon,
using a running stitch. *Start your basting on an
edge with a seam to secure.*

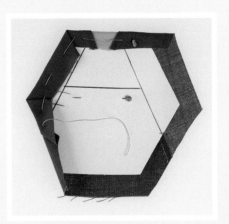

Basted Hexie, back side

⊗ **Do not** remove the pin until at least 3 sides are
basted.

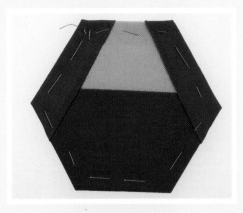

Basted Hexie, front side

How to Join Rosettes

1. Lay out your rosette in the arrangement desired.

2. Hold 2 Hexies together, rights sides touching and edges lined up.

3. Knot the end of your sewing thread. Run your needle about½" from one corner. This will place your knot away from the corner and reduce bulk.

4. Take 2 stitches in the corner to secure it. Make small whip stitches to just catch the edges of the fabric. Try not to sew through the paper.

5. Now open up the Hexies so they lay flat, and continue to sew. Gently run the needle through the fabric and across the paper. No stitches show on the front.

6. When you reach the next corner, add on another Hexie and continue sewing. Be sure to secure the corner by double stitching there.

Arranging the Rosette

Now we'll show you some ways to arrange your Hexies into rosettes (groups of 7 Hexies).

Boomer Original

  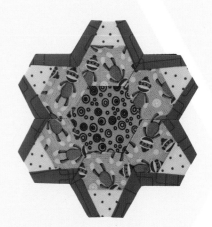

Boomer Variation 1

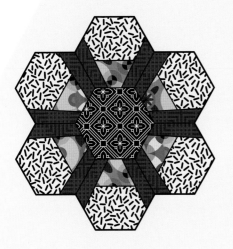  

Boomer Variation 2

Boomer Variation 3

 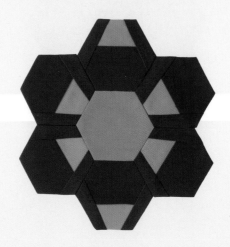 

Boomer Variation 4

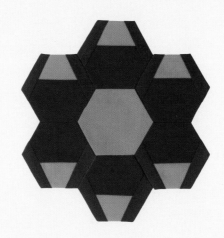
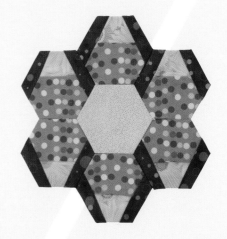

Boomer Variation 5

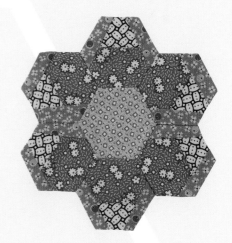

Boomer Variation 6

Adding Hexies to the Quilt Top

Appliqué

Note: We used needle turn by hand appliqué method to construct our samples. Any method of appliqué can be used. Please adapt the following guidelines to work with your chosen method.

1. Gently press your entire rosette while basting stitches are still in place. DO NOT use steam or hold the iron on the rosette for too long — the paper will warp and not be reusable.

2. Remove the basting stitches from the center Hexie of the rosette. Spray with starch. Press.

3. One at a time, remove the basting stitches from each "petal Hexie" of the rosette. Spray with starch, press. Remove the paper (save it for another project).

4. Pin your rosette on an open area of the quilt top. The rosettes can be placed on point or on their side.

5. Appliqué the edges of the rosette in place by hand.

6. Remove the background fabric behind the appliquéd rosette to reduce bulk. Cut away the background, leaving a generous ¼" seam allowance. (Note: this is not possible if you use a fusible method for appliqué.)

7. Repeat this process for the other rosettes.

Finishing

And that famous last statement: quilt as desired and bind!

A large bed size quilt is easily made by simply repeating the wallhanging pattern four times and sewing it together as a large four patch.